Donald English

An Evangelical Celebration

Edited by
Ronald W. Abbott

An Evangelical Celebration

HEADLINE SPECIAL

Published for **Headway** by
MOORLEY'S Print & Publishing

British Library Cataloguing in Publication Data.
A catalogue record for this book is available
from the British Library.

ISBN 0 86071 530 2

Published for **Headway** by

MOORLEY'S Print & Publishing

23 Park Rd., Ilkeston, Derbys DE7 5DA
Tel/Fax: (0115) 932 0643

CONTRIBUTORS

The Rev. **Alan Warrell** M.A.(Cantab) B.A.(Lond) is the retired Chairman of the Shetland District. After serving for several years in Nigeria with the Missionary Society, he has also served in circuits in the West Midlands and the South East.

Mrs **Margaret Allwood** is a member of Farnsfield Methodist Church, near Mansfield. She is also a Local Preacher in her Circuit.

The Rev. **Leo Osborn** is a minister in the North Shields and Whitley Bay Circuit at the Church where Donald and Bertha English were stationed for six years.

The Rev. **Paul Smith** M.A. (Manch.) is Superintendent of the Altrincham Circuit in Cheshire and the current Chairman of Headway.

The Rev. **David King** is Superintendent of Plymouth Central Hall, Devon.

Mrs **Margaret Parker** is Vice President of the Methodist Conference for the year 1998- 1999. She comes from Cheadle Hulme, Cheshire and is a specialist in organising and writing about small groups in the day to day life of the church.

The Rev. Dr. **Joe Hale** is General Secretary of the World Methodist Council, based at Lake Junaluska, North Carolina, U.S.A.

The Rev. **Martin Turner** is Superintendent Minister of the Hemel Hempstead and Berkhamsted Circuit, and until recently, Chairman of Headway.

The Rev. **Richard M. Andrew** B.A. (Lond) is Minister at Endcliffe Methodist Church, in the Eccleshall Circuit, Sheffield.

The Rev. **Brian Hoare** B.D.(Lond)   a past President of Conference is currently a member of the Connexional Team with a responsibility for Evangelism, and based at Central Hall, Westminster.

The Rev. Dr. **Billy Graham** is himself!

The Editor, Mr. **Ron Abbott** Bsc.Dip. Theol.(Lond) was Lay Tutor and Senior Tutor at Cliff College, 1982-1992.

Preface

When the Headway leadership asked me to put together tributes to Donald English I did not envisage quite how big a task that was going to be.

Mary and I first knew Donald as fellow students at University College, Leicester. We have been firm friends to him, and then to his wife Bertha, and the family, ever since.

What vivid memories we all have - of Donald's humour, his sporting prowess, his care, his prayer life, his God-given leadership, his incisive mind, his preaching and teaching. What follows tells story after story of the kind of man Donald was.

His appeal was world wide, and across the denominational divide. Many of us who worked with him at Leicester realised that he would go far. The reflections in this publication show how, in an even broader sense, this all came about, and with a bigger team than we could have ever imagined, working for the Kingdom of God. What an international team he led!

As a man he had an amazing capacity to relate to friends he had not seen for years. One letter from a former Leicester student illustrates this:-

"We found it remarkable when we just turned up a few years ago at a Spurgeon's College garden party, not knowing that Don would be there, and immediately he walked across to us, recognising our aged faces, calling out our names, embracing us and making us feel like long lost family - such was his gift for people contact. . ."

The number of people, ministerial, and lay who have been encouraged by a brief conversation with Donald must be without number. In the following brief chapters you will read over and over again about his grasp of theological ideas and their application to day to day evangelism.

When he was honoured by Leicester University I went to listen to his masterful lecture on "John Wesley - Reverend, Revivalist or Revolutionary."

A former Conference representative recalls how he turned a crucial debate by making a strong plea for "more Bible in the argument." The report went back for a re-think.

It is good to see ourselves as others see us, and the comments from Dr's Billy Graham and Joe Hale are revealing.

I have been thrilled, inspired and encouraged by all the words sent to me in recent weeks. Donald was indeed one of "The Greats" of Methodism in the second half of the 20th Century.

> "Finish then thy new creation,
> Pure and spotless let us be;
> Let us see thy great salvation,
> Perfectly restored in Thee:
> Changed from glory into glory,
> Till in heaven we take our place,
> Till we cast our crowns before Thee,
> Lost in wonder, love and praise."
>
> Charles Wesley.

March 1999

Ron Abbott.
Editor – Headline

Introduction

Donald English has had a great influence upon many of our lives. After attending the Westminster thanksgiving service and reading the obituaries I realised how much more could have been said.

At the time I was Chair of Headway and I suggested at an Executive Committee meeting that several essays of tribute might be helpful to many. This idea was enthusiastically received, and Don would have been delighted that his good friend since Leicester student days, Ron Abbott, took on the work of editing such a booklet.

Two concerns have been raised about this project.

The FIRST is that Don's life and ministry warrant far more than a small book of essays. That is quite right. We hope and pray that a worthy biography will soon be written. This booklet, which purports to be no more, is just an immediate response from friends to a man who meant much.

The SECOND concern is that these essays come largely from the evangelical stable. We make no apologies for this. The thanksgiving service was quite rightly the celebration of the whole Church, thanking God for the life of a distinguished leader. However Don was at heart an evangelical Christian, and we wanted to celebrate that and make our own particular appraisal of one who was very much "our" leader as evangelicals. This small booklet is the result.

Our thanks must go to Paul and Richard English for allowing us to go ahead, and of course we have such happy memories of Bertha, always Don's supportive wife.

All profits from this book are to be given to the Evangelical Forum for Theology and will be used to set up a bursary fund in memory of Donald which will enable evangelical Methodist students to take further opportunities for study.

Martin Turner.

The Rev. Alan Warrell, retired Chairman of the Shetland District of the Methodist Church, reflects on the early years of Donald English.

Donald English - Student

I met Don English when I went up to University College, Leicester in 1949 and that appears somehow to qualify me to write about his student days. I have however contacted a number of friends and colleagues who knew him both at Leicester and Cambridge and I trust that what follows is a faithful reflection of what they have shared with me. The more I have learnt the more I have come to appreciate what a privilege has been ours to have known Don. It is not an understatement to say that he touched many lives whilst he was still a student and these were his formative years!

Donald English was born on the 20th July 1930 at Consett in County Durham the only son of Robert and Ena English. Don, as we all knew him, was blessed with a shock of red hair but his nickname at school was "The Duke". He was blessed in that he was born into a Christian family who attended the High Westwood Methodist Chapel in Consett. His mother was a gentle person and Don inherited much from her. She was also a member of the local dramatic society and no doubt this made its mark upon him too.

Don's schooling began in 1935 at Leadgate Infant School. When the family moved to Delves Lane in 1937 he attended the Delves Lane Infant and Junior School. Here Jack Gair, his junior schoolteacher, had a great influence upon him. He recognised his potential, taught him to believe in himself, and equipped him to go on in 1941 to Consett Grammar School, a three-mile walk to and from school each day. His own reflections of his time at Grammar School always suggested that he did not get on too well with Mr. French the Maths teacher. Don's ability to rehearse the Saturday football results passed unrewarded. However he obtained his School Certificate and Higher School Certificate as they were then, and in 1948 entered University College Leicester to read History.

Back at the High Westwood Chapel Don pumped the organ for his Uncle George Weston who was organist there. When the family moved to Delves Lane they attended the Middle Street Church in the town centre. This was the Circuit Church and the great attraction for Don was the soccer team which the 10th. Consett Boys' Brigade Company ran. He played outside right for them.

However it was during the ministry of the Rev. Frank Ward at Consett (1942 - 1947) that Don felt the challenge of the Gospel. There were two men in the church who had a particular influence upon him at this time. They were 'Big'

Bill, a Coal Board clerk, who stood 6 foot 6 inches tall and weighed 20 stones, and Matt Wigham, both Local Preachers. They had been in the War and their witness impressed Don. The Rev. Benjamin Drewery had conducted a Boys' Brigade Enrolment Service and Don had been made a Corporal. At the end of the service Mr. Drewery made an appeal for commitment to Christ. To Don's amazement a lad whom he looked up to and one he counted as a Christian went forward. At the After-Service Bill and Matt gave their testimonies and when the appeal was made Don made his response. He could do no other.

Don's preaching began in 1949 when he was home from College. The Rev. Benjamin Drewery asked Don whether he was free that Sunday night to come with him to Castleside. On the bus he suggested that Don just give out the hymns and read the lessons. This was extended into leading the prayers, and when Mr. Drewery, feeling unwell, had to leave the pulpit to go into the vestry, Don had to preach as well. It's recorded that that first sermon set forth the whole counsel of God and included a sweep from Genesis to Revelation all in a matter of minutes. When Mr. Drewery returned he preached for a further 40 minutes!

It was back at University that Don gained experience preaching in the Leicester South Circuit with the student preaching team and also in the Leicester Market Place on a Sunday night after evening worship.

Don entered University College Leicester in September 1948 and came under the influence of Professor Simmonds, Head of the History Department. He was a fine historian and an interesting lecturer and Don, who had a passion for books and learning and study, made steady progress with his studies gaining a London B.A. Second Class Upper Division after three years. He then entered the Education Department and gained a Credit in his Graduate's Certificate of Education. Subsequently the University honoured him with an Honorary Doctor of Literature whilst Convocation elected him Graduate for the Year in 1988. He responded with the Convocation Lecture entitled "John Wesley; Reverend, Revivalist or Revolutionary?"

But of Don's student days at Leicester there is more to tell. On the football field Don's skill won him a place in the College team as right back and captain, touring with them in Germany in 1951. He also played for the Universities' Athletic Union and trained with Leicester City FC, who with Sunderland United FC were interested in him as a Professional Player. He was called for a trial for the England International Amateur Team as Full Back but the existing Captain held that position!

There was another trial and this was on a Sunday but like Eric Liddell he felt he had to decline. This caused later reflective heart-searching.

Don joined the College Christian Union when he arrived at Leicester. The C.U. numbered about 70 members in a College of 700 under-graduates which by its nature was a fairly tightly knit community. So it was that Don with George Measures and Tony Davies, organised Freshers' Socials and End of Term entertainment with great success. Don's spiritual stature was quickly recognised and he was soon "Publications Secretary", i.e. Book Steward, on the C.U. Committee. He served in its leadership throughout his Leicester days being President in 1951-1952. The Publications Secretary had outreach opportunities. As well as looking after a selection of Inter-Varsity Fellowship books (IVP today) which Don carried around on his back from his digs, he brought them for sale at Open Meetings. There was also a book-table set up in the College Crush Hall once a week. It was through this that contact was made with other students. Don was always an evangelist and on one occasion at a Student's Union Debate he opposed the motion put by Bryan Wilson, who later became a fellow of All Souls, Oxford and a distinguished writer on the Sociology of religion. The proposition was that "This House does not believe in an After Life". Needless to say this caught the interest of the whole College and whilst Don spoke the C.U. prayed. The motion was defeated.

When a Mission was proposed to the University Don became the obvious choice for Mission Committee Chairman. The University motto is "Ut Vitam Habeant" and John 10. verse 10 became the natural theme. The Rev. the Hon. Roland Lamb was invited to be the main missioner. Roland Lamb was a Methodist minister and at that time was an I.V.F. Travelling Secretary. He was to have an impact which influenced the direction of many lives for God. His regular visits to the College introduced the Methodists to the Revival Fellowship - recently formed. But of greater significance was the number who subsequently offered for the Christian ministry - six became Methodist ministers - and many others dedicated themselves to home and overseas service.

A group from the C.U. joined the I.V.F. Camp at Keswick in 1953 and Don spent sleepless hours wrestling with the "Holiness" teaching and "The Second Blessing". That year too, the C.U. held a Mission in West Ham based on the vicarage. Don is remembered for his care of a very difficult child. There were other Colleges in Leicester and with other members of the C.U. Don brought about L.I.C.C.U. (Leicester Inter-Collegiate Christian Union) linking the University College with the Domestic Science College, the Teacher Training College, the Technical College, and the Speech Therapy College. There was a wider gathering of Midland College Christian Unions and in 1952 Don became the Midland Representative on the Executive Committee of the I.V.F. He became responsible for organising the termly conferences.

Don's digs during the Leicester days were in Wigston and on a Sunday he worshipped at the Frederick Street Methodist Church in the morning and in the evening at Clarendon Park Methodist Church in Leicester, the student church. After evening worship an 'At Home Hour' was hosted by the church for all who would come - and a lot of students did. Here after a friendly cup of tea there would be a speaker or some special event organised by the church. Needless to say this was where Don was often found.

However his evangelical heart drew him to the Leicester Market Place some Sunday evenings, and one day he found himself being told that he was the next to speak. He did, and so began an open-air ministry alongside the Student Preaching Team which went out into the Leicester South Circuit encouraged by the Revs. Sydney Gordon, Ronald E. South and Willoughby Thompson.

Those who knew Don in Leicester all speak of someone who was head and shoulders above his fellow Christians. He was someone with spiritual insight and he already had a great understanding of the Bible. He was very thorough at committee work. He also had a great awareness of the tensions between different theological positions. The books in his extensive library reflected the breadth of his studies. He wore a Scripture Union badge in one lapel and an M.A.Y.C. one in the other! He had a remarkable way of giving you his whole attention and always there was time for prayer.

Leaving Leicester in 1953 Don did his National Service in the R.A.F. as an Education Officer. Flying Officer English continued to play football often being flown to his matches. It was during this time that he completed his Local Preacher training, being received on to Full Plan at Consett in 1954.

After his two years in the Forces Don became a Travelling Secretary for the I.V.F. working in the Midlands and the North of England. He visited colleges and led missions and lives were touched. It was during this time that he felt the call into the Methodist ministry and he began the candidating process. In 1958 having passed the various examinations he appeared before the "July" Committee who appeared to have given him a rough passage particularly over the Doctrine of Substitutionary Atonement. However Conference accepted him and in September 1958 he entered Wesley House Cambridge. Two years were spent at Cambridge studying for the Tripos Part 2 under such ministers as W.F. Flemington, Philip Watson & Michael Skinner and Owen Chadwick. There was time for soccer as well and each Wednesday afternoon a training session was held on Jesus Green under Don who was the captain of the House Team. The College team drew both against Handsworth and Richmond Colleges in the annual Methodist matches in the two years Don was at Cambridge. However he and two others from the House did play with the

Fitzwilliam team (Wesley House and Fitzwilliam House are affiliated) and on that occasion they won the Cambridge Inter-College Cup, a feat never accomplished before. A special dinner was given in honour of the three Housemen! Don also showed his prowess at table tennis. It was during this time that he began to suffer with his back. Don applied himself to the study of the Greek New Testament and mastered the language so well that the Principal, the Rev. J.F Flemington had Don tutor the slow learners. Being older and more experienced than some of the other Housemen and with a quiet dry sense of humour Don played a leading role in the life of the House and in due course became Chairman. His major contribution was in the realm of prayer. Three times a week at the end of the day the M.R.F. members met for prayer. These meetings were more like a Class Meeting. During the time he was Chairman Don sought to establish a prayer group on each staircase. He played his part as the Houseman in a Meth-Soc. group which gave wider contact in the University as did membership of C.I.C.C.U. (Cambridge Inter-Collegiate Christian Union) which met every day for prayer. His contact with John Stott when as an I.V.F. Travelling Secretary led to the establishment at this time of summer house parties on the wild windswept coast of Pembrokeshire for ex-Leicester friends and others. He led these at first, and they still continue.

While still at Wesley House he co-operated with Howard Marshall in the production of "Christian Belief" for the I.V.F. and wrote in the Wesley House Magazine on "These Fundamentalists!", always a talking point at the House. In 1960 he sat the Cambridge Tripos and was awarded an Upper Second, or 2.1.

Looking back to those days, those who shared them with him speak of Don's openness and friendship and his loving concern for people. In many ways Don was always a student - from 1960 to 1962 he was Assistant Tutor at Wesley College, Headingly, Leeds. From 1962 to 1965, he was Tutor at the Union Theological College at Umuahia in Eastern Nigeria where he led his students on mission in various circuits. Returning from Nigeria Don became minister of the Broadway Church in Cullercoats until 1972. He was then appointed by Conference to Hartley Victoria College in Manchester moving in 1973 to Wesley College, Bristol to teach Practical Theology and Methodism. In 1982 he moved to Westminster to become General Secretary of the Methodist Home Mission Division.

During these years he continued his studies and wrote a number of books. Constantly in demand as a Bible teacher world-wide, he received recognition for his scholarship by several universities in this country and abroad. As someone wrote, "A Bible study with Don was to learn and grow. His

12

knowledge was never an academic thing but a personal and intimate passion for Jesus". Always humble, always approachable, a smile and an encouragement - this was Don the student, and the man. They said at Clarendon Park when he was a third year student that he was a future President of the Conference and they were right.

Mrs Margaret Allwood, a Methodist from Farnsfield, Notts tells her own story of the PRAYER SUPPORT provided for Donald.

Donald English - Man of Prayer

Donald English was not aware at first, exactly how much the Lord went before him in preparation for what were to be the greatest years of his ministry. God decided to enlist some extra help with regard to prayer support for him...

In 1977 while Donald was serving as a tutor at Wesley College, Bristol I was being given the vision to set up a prayer chain. My Christian neighbour took me to the Cliff College Celebration on Spring Bank Holiday Monday for the first time. All I saw of the speaker was the back of a dark head and suit; but I heard his message and determined I would be back. I returned in July for the Derwent Week. There he was again - Donald English. This time he gave his testimony. A few weeks before, we had heard that he was to be President of the Conference. Being a new Christian I did not understand what that meant, but I was told we should pray for him.

"Pray for him!" These words stuck in my mind together with his name. I couldn't get rid of them. So I prayed for him. Not knowing very well how to pray and not knowing Donald English I just asked the Lord to bless him. Increasingly I felt I must get others to pray for him. I started a prayer-chain asking people to lift him up before the Lord for the same five minutes every day, starting at 8am and continuing till 10pm just to cover him when he was President of the Conference, and starting straight away. The idea was quickly approved and many names flowed in. Then Satan discouraged me. I felt like giving up. Protests from my friends persuaded me to keep going. I prayed and thought about it very much. Then I felt a great burden to pray for him in public meetings, i.e. Bible studies, but I was afraid. Eventually I prayed again. I asked -"Lord there must be more to it than this? Please help me!"

Immediately, God gave me John ch.12. v.32 "and I, if I be lifted up from the earth, will draw all men unto me."

He reminded me of the story of Moses lifting up his arms. When they were raised the Israelites were winning, and when they fell the enemy Amalekites prevailed (Ex.ch.17 v.11). Aaron and Hur "held up his hands... and his hands were steady until the sun set."

It was so exciting! This really confirmed everything for me. The Rev. Donald English would lift up the Lord, all over the country as he was President, and we would "hold up his hands until the sun set." (10pm) with our prayer timetable. If we were faithful, while his arms were up, people would be drawn to the Lord - revival would come. Reassured, I set to work on the timetable again. I calculated I would need 168 names to fill the whole prayer chain of 5 minute intervals for 14 hours. I was told I should go to the M.R.F. Conference (Methodist Revival Prayer Fellowship) because they would be interested. Sure enough when I told their Annual General Meeting about it, a long queue of people waited to become a part of it. After that, I went to the Keswick Convention, the Cliff Celebration, the Derwent Week and many other places besides. I circulated four copies of the testimony given at Cliff.

I must tell you at this point that not only Methodists were on the timetable but also Anglicans, Brethren, Pentecostals, Baptists, Church of the Nazarene, they all joyfully joined in. This is how the prayer chain for Donald English began. It was not until a year later that I actually met Rev. Donald English face to face, at the M.R.F. (now Headway) Prayer Conference.

He was the President by then and to my surprise he had already heard about the prayer-chain. He said it was very humbling but he agreed to send me his itinerary and a prayer letter. Shortly before all this when I had first become a Christian, I bought a small second-hand typewriter and prayed, "Here I am Lord, I can type, what do you want me to do?"

Now I knew. I typed out the itinerary and letter, with carbon paper, enough copies for everyone (several hundred) four times a year. Nearly every name represented a church, a fellowship, a family or a college as well as many individuals.

As years passed and technology developed it was, of course, done on a computer and photocopier. Cheques, postal orders, stamps, cash, envelopes were all sent at different times by different people to finance it all! Wonderful!

The prayer chain went on for 20 years, during which time some members have died, some who were "the young folk" when we began, have married, some to each other and a few have become Methodist ministers. Also, new people have joined us at various stages along the way. Donald moved on from being just Rev. Donald English to Rev. Dr. Donald English MA, he moved from being a tutor in a Methodist college to being President of Conference TWICE (The only person to do that since 1932) to become General Secretary of the Home Missions Division, Moderator of the Free Church Federal Council and Chairman of the World Methodist Council with a great many other things in between. He preached before the Queen, Princes, and Members of Parliament, travelled the world more than once, headed missions and conferences and spoke regularly on Radio Four's "Thought for the Day" and sometimes on TV, not to mention the on-going ministry of tapes and videos and his book writing. But he always found the time to write to his faithful prayer warriors.

Over the years it meant a great deal to Dr. English to have this prayer support and he repeatedly thanked and encouraged us in it, telling us how he felt physically upheld. He used to tell me also that he could testify to the power which God gave to his preaching and ministry as a result of the prayers of the people. He said that he was particularly conscious of it in the big moments. As broadcasting opportunities developed Donald said he was thankful for the sense of not walking the road alone.

Above all, with each letter he sent, he requested that we pray for his beloved family. He did not leave the work of prayer to others. Bertha his wife once told me that he was up very early each morning to have his own prayer time. What moved me most was when he told me that he prayed for me.

I will always be grateful to God for allowing me the privilege of being a small part of the administration of the wonderful ministry of this very special man of God.

The Rev. Leo Osborn is minister of Cullercoats Methodist Church in the North-east where Donald English was minister on his return from Nigeria, and before he moved to teach in our Methodist colleges. His words also include comments from Bill Flewker who was Senior Steward when the English family were in Cullercoats.

Donald English - Pastor

It was in 1966 that Donald English became minister of Cullercoats Methodist Church in the North Shields and Whitley Bay Circuit, nine miles north-east of Newcastle. He remained there for six years before moving to Hartley Victoria College, Manchester. Cullercoats proved to be Don's only circuit appointment so I have asked Bill Flewker who was Senior Church Steward during Don's ministry here to write a few words about Don as Pastor. "A pastor is someone who exercises spiritual guidance and Donald English certainly did that in so many different ways. He could not do anything else for that was the way he was, and that was the way he lived, because of his belief and love of his Lord. During his ministry at Cullercoats this showed in whatever he did, both in general pastoral oversight or in particular cases. This pastoral oversight extended much further, for if he felt that an individual needed urging to pursue, or not to pursue, a particular course of action he would not hesitate to make his views known but always in a positive and kindly way. Your problems became his problems and together a solution was so often found. In spite of having a large congregation he knew the vast majority by name and his personal touch and greeting made one feel special. One of the aspects of this care was the fact that each day he would set aside time to pray for a certain number of church members and so work his way through the membership.

The pastoral care was never more evident than with young people, with whom he could communicate at their level, and about their interests. The fact that they would meet regularly each Sunday evening at Don and Bertha's home created an atmosphere where it was possible to discuss and debate any topic, religious or secular, with complete freedom of opinion, and where valuable advice was always available. His guidance, encouragement and support helped many youngsters to focus their thoughts and hopes for the future. This influence often extended long after they had left home for college etc., and well into adult life. Alongside this interest in young people he was equally concerned with the spiritual life of every section of the church and would constantly challenge and encourage individuals and groups. As a direct consequence of this there was a real growth in the spiritual life of the church which resulted in an increased awareness and concern for others. This showed itself in so many ways, and indeed, remains a legacy which is still bearing fruit. His pastoral care for the sick, the bereaved and those in any kind of need was exceptional and he gave unstintingly of his time, comfort and support, made sure that the housebound and members with prolonged illness or in hospital received regular communion."

Don returned to Cullercoats on a number of occasions in the following years, the last just a few weeks after Bertha had died. The strain and tiredness showed in his face and having to talk to so many people who knew him and Bertha so well, in a place where they had been so happy, proved very hard indeed. Yet Don was the last person to leave the church premises that evening and even then walked home talking of one whom he had never met before but who was going through a spiritual crisis and had turned to him for support. A true pastor indeed!

I first met Don when he became tutor at Wesley College, Bristol in 1973. Those of us who were evangelicals rejoiced at his appointment perhaps fondly imagining that we would be given an easy ride. We were soon to be disillusioned! The first essay he set was on God as Creator and Redeemer. As a good sound evangelical I wrote about 1450 words on God as Redeemer with many and varied references to the cross and about three lines on God as Creator with many and varied references to nothing at all. When the essay was returned the red pen had been used in abundance and most of what I had written had been torn to shreds! Annoyed and embarrassed in equal measure I sought Don out wondering perhaps if he was as sound as I had been led to believe. It was then that I saw for the first time how Don was able to excel both as theologian and pastor at the same time. He explained firmly how my view of God was lop-sided, he taught me in five minutes in simple yet profound language more about God's purposes in creation and incarnation than I'd learnt in twenty-one years previously. He reminded me that if I thought the purpose of his presence in Bristol was to affirm evangelicals in their narrowness then I'd better think again ... and then he said how thrilled he was that I was one of his students, that he'd always be there at any time to offer counsel and advice (which he was), that he would pray for me (and did so there and then) and finally handed me a form to join C.E.I.M. (which I did!)

This firmness and gentleness which was Donald English's pastoral approach was seen time and again by all the students in his care. When I arrived back late for prayers after driving through the night on my way home from Hartlepool (Aston Villa Open Air Revival Meeting!) he tore me off a strip ... before asking me whether it was a good game and who scored and how pleased he was I'd visited the North-East etc etc. And when I foolishly made some joke about having seen one of his books in a "remainders" shop he

18

didn't hesitate to show me how hurt he was by such a comment. He wasn't altogether displeased when I presented him with the copy to give to someone else!

When Don eventually moved on to the Home Mission Division and twice became President of Conference, the great thing about him was that he never allowed high office to make him inaccessible. How many Methodists in general and evangelicals in particular sought his counsel, help, and advice no one can begin to calculate but when it came it was always from a pastor's heart firm, gentle, encouraging, challenging and above all in love. In short, Donald English was an answer to the often sung prayer of Charles Wesley: -

> "(Lord) collect thy flock and give them food,
> and pastors after thine own heart".

We thank God for Him.

The Rev. Paul Smith is Superintendent of the Altrincham Circuit, current Chairman of Headway and a regular speaker at gatherings, large and small.

Donald English - Preacher

At 7.15pm on Wednesday 15th April 1998 Donald English took his place on the stage at Easter People in The Opera House, Blackpool where he was to be the guest preacher. Fifteen minutes earlier he had joined the worship leaders in one of the dressing rooms. They were already engaged in prayer when Donald arrived. Without a word the coat was cast aside, the brief case placed on the floor and then he knelt on the carpet as the events of that evening were offered to the Lord. Anyone who saw him kneeling there knew that for him it was a familiar position. Here was a man who knew what it was to go to people for God and go to God for the people.

As the meeting began he gave himself to the worship. He was still mourning the death of Bertha, his dear wife, and the singing of 'I will sing the wondrous story' moved him very deeply. Those who had crowded into the theatre that night could not see the tears well in his eyes as we sang the chorus. I was standing next to him and when the hymn was over and we took our seats I simply enquired whether all was well. 'Yes', he replied, 'it was "the crystal sea" that did it.' When he was formally introduced the whole theatre erupted in spontaneous applause. In his typical self-effacing way he was embarrassed by it, but no one could doubt the love and respect in which he was held. During the hymn before his message he made his way to the lectern. The Bible was placed upon it, and then the notes, although he never needed them. During the last verse his head was bowed in prayer and those large freckled hands were clasped just beneath his chin. There were several deep breaths and as the congregation took their seats everyone knew why they were there. Donald's words, rooted in the word of scripture, became the word of God to them.

To say that Donald English was a fine Biblical expositor is to state the obvious. As an evangelical Christian he held the Bible in high regard. Like Wesley, he was a man of one book. The clarity of his exposition left his hearers wondering why they had read that passage so often and never grasped its heart before, but it belied the tremendous amount of preparation which such exposition demands. Donald knew that in order to get to the heart of a passage of scripture any preacher must grasp the impact it made on those who first heard its teaching or read its message. He would seek to get inside their minds and hearts. As he preached the hearer was left in no doubt that here was someone who knew as much as possible about the writer and the cultural and historic situation of those who first read it. This wealth of information was not disgorged in the preaching, but if the preaching was to be effective it had to be assimilated during the preparation.

Donald knew that it takes far more than a clear understanding of the scriptures to be an effective preacher. His acknowledged effectiveness indicates that he was familiar with both the ancient world of the Bible and the world in which his hearers had to live out their discipleship. He read voraciously and even a cursory glance at his bookshelves indicates his keen desire to understand the pressures under which people live and the forces which shape contemporary society.

He had the ability to identify trends, analyse forces and grasp issues. Convinced as he was that there is no situation in which the gospel has nothing to say, he would bring his understanding of the biblical message to bear on his understanding of society and personal need in a way which convinced his hearers that he really understood them, their needs and the difference which the gospel could make. Maybe that is why he endeared himself to so many. He knew what made people tick. He knew the power of God's grace in Christ; and he never lost sight of the transformation which can occur when the two are brought together.

Probably everyone who heard Donald English preach can remember at least one of his illustrations. They were always singularly appropriate. Like his Master, Donald told simple stories to make profound truth understandable to ordinary people. He observed everything and, often at his own expense, would relate an incident which illuminated the point with a clarity that could not be missed. The fact that sometimes the stories came up more than once did not matter! Even if you got to the punch line before him the story was just as powerful. He could place an abstract concept in a concrete situation so that ordinary people would understand it; and they did.

For Donald English, the gospel truth was so fundamental that it demanded a response. No one could sit under his preaching and remain neutral. The truth of scripture forced the hearer into making a decision, and Donald was never afraid of asking them to do so. There must be thousands of people all over the world who recognise that, under God, it was Donald English who brought them to a moment of decision. Like many evangelicals before him, Donald knew the importance of moving the body to signify a movement of the soul. It was during one of his Presidential years that Donald made the British Methodist people more familiar with 'the altar call' which had long been a tradition in American Methodism.

As the closing hymn was sung people would make their way, with great reverence, to the communion rail. There they would kneel and in silent prayer make their peace with God. As the hymn continued they would return to their seats; outwardly the same but inwardly renewed by the grace of God. No one could doubt that they were encountering God in that moment, and it was through Donald English's ministry.

Philip Brooks spoke of preaching as "the communication of truth through personality". It was one of Donald's favourite definitions. He did not model himself on any other preacher, even though he learned from them. He was just 'Donald', which is why people loved him so. To see him preaching was to observe someone who was completely consumed by the wonder of his message. The message possessed his whole being and he gave himself to the privilege of preaching without reserve. Any congregation who sat under Donald English's ministry not only heard the gospel, they saw one who embodied it. Through his preaching the clarity of truth mingled with the constraint of love so that ordinary people felt drawn to Christ. We thank God for everyone who was drawn closer to Christ through the preaching ministry of Donald English.

We had just finished singing one of Charles Wesley's great hymns as we stood on the stage at Easter People. As we turned to take our seats Donald looked out over the sea of faces before us. He turned to me, "Remember what Moody said," he whispered, "It's worth living for this!". He was right.

The Rev. David King, Superintendent of Plymouth Central Hall, writes from his experiences of mission with Donald.

Donald English - Evangelist.

"He was a Christian in the conservative evangelical tradition:
**committed to Christ and therefore committed to Scripture as God's Word;
committed to Christ and therefore committed to lead others to Him.**"

These words were used by the Rev. Professor Peter Stephens, President of the Methodist Conference 1998-1999, at a Service of Thanksgiving held for the life of Donald English at Westminster Central Hall. The President affirmed so much of Donald's gifting as an evangelist. My first meeting with Donald was as a student at Wesley College, Bristol. Outside the normal timetable, Donald taught evangelism to those of us with a particular interest. Evangelism seemed to be something of a sideline, despised by some, but during his ministry he has been used by God to move evangelism in Methodism and the wider Church back on to the agenda in a serious way.

He was no "soloist" in evangelism, and always wanted to be part of a team. He was overjoyed when a boy belonging to a church in Loughton, Essex, (where we were on Mission together) asked his Headmaster if the mission team visiting his church could come along to a school assembly and share the Christian message. Along with the team, Donald went with great enthusiasm, giving thanks to God for the initiative of the boy. At local church city-wide initiatives, major gatherings, and at international events, his evangelism usually sprang from Biblical exposition. It has been said that Donald turned everything he did into evangelism. As he had taught his students, he kept one foot in the Biblical context and the other in the modern world. When challenging people with the claims of Christ he encouraged the engagement of the mind. His scholarship and outstanding use of illustrations enriched his work as an evangelist. He had the capacity both to proclaim the faith to those not yet converted, and to teach and encourage Christians in the same presentation.

Donald communicated with business, civic, national and international leaders, and also with very "ordinary" people. It was recently said that "when he preached to thousands you thought he was just talking to you". At a weekend mission based in Blackpool, through Donald, the call of Christ came to a young man. The young man faced very major decisions in his life. With his usual sensitivity, Donald invited people to make a public response. Swiftly the young man moved from the back of the balcony to the communion rail.

This was an occasion of life-giving and life-changing proportion - not an isolated experience in Donald's ministry as an evangelist.

Donald was not interested in crowds, but in individuals. Whenever possible after a mission he would record, or ask for, the names of those for whom the occasion had been of major significance so that he could pray for them. What a prayer list he and Bertha must have had! He saw evangelism as part of the whole ministry of Christ. This was the principle highlighted in the contribution to the publication *"Sharing in God's Mission"*.

Through preaching, teaching and writing he made evangelism credible to many for whom it had not been. Throughout much of his ministry Donald was a regular visitor to Plymouth. Had he not been taken to glory he would have led the work at the Plymouth Methodist Central Hall for a twelve-month period. Without a doubt there would have been a particular emphasis on evangelism. His ministry in Plymouth was very much wider than the Central Hall.

Two of his major city-wide U.K. missions were held in Plymouth - "Power for Life" in 1976 and more recently "Making Waves," in 1997, based on the "One Voice" mission he had led in York in 1992. Donald was the main speaker for "Making Waves". This was to be his last major mission. Prebendary John Watson, former Vicar of St. Andrew's Parish Church in Plymouth City Centre, who worked closely with Donald on both occasions, reflecting on the "Power for Life" Mission, regarded it as of major significance, especially the evangelistic talks Donald had given which were held in St. Andrews at lunchtime. He described Donald as a man with "his head in the heavens and his feet on the ground, and with a real grip on the human situation". He tells of the crowd of business people, starting with approximately 200 people on the Monday, and growing to about 600 people by the end of the week. This speaks for itself. As an evangelist, John Watson held Donald in the highest regard, and believes "that had he been a member of the established Church he would have been at the top".

Donald encouraged the widest possible denominational involvement in evangelism, longing that all, from the House Churches to the Roman Catholic Church, should work together in proclaiming the faith of Christ crucified and risen. A Roman Catholic Christian described Donald's evangelism as "gentle but powerful, rooted in our day to day experience, respectful of each individual and of all Christian traditions. Sharing himself and his love for the Lord, he drew many to the Lord, and transformed lives."

One of the greatest gifts Donald had was the capacity to be trusted by leaders and people of the widest possible grouping of Christian denominations. With their confidence he proclaimed the Gospel to thousands on their behalf. This he did in "Making Waves", held in the Plymouth Pavilions, one of the South West's largest venues, where thousands flocked for eight nights. Each night, without notes, Donald "commended Christ". No other event has attracted so many people for so many consecutive nights to this huge venue.

Like his Lord, Donald proclaimed to thousands, but he had a heart and time for individuals. He encouraged all to share in witnessing to Christ, and longed for more within the life of the Church to share in the work of an evangelist.

Mrs Margaret Parker was elected Vice-President of the Methodist Conference for the year 1998-99. Having spent many years as a Conference representative and a member of many committees, she willingly agreed to write about this aspect of Donald's life.

Donald English - Statesman

Donald English's statesmanship ran like a thread through many facets of his life and work. I mention four of those facets.

1. **British Methodism** in which Donald had the distinction of being President of the Methodist Conference in 1978 and again in 1990, the only person to be elected President twice since Methodist Union in 1932. He taught in three British Methodist theological colleges, in Leeds, Manchester and Bristol. He was the founding chair of Conservative Evangelicals in Methodism. And perhaps best known of all, he served as General Secretary of the Methodist Home Mission Division from 1982 until his retirement in 1995.

2. His statesmanlike qualities were demonstrated on the **World Methodist scene**. He served on the World Methodist Council Executive for many years, and chaired the WMC from 1991 - 1996. He spoke with world leaders, including P.W. Botha in South Africa, and Pope John Paul II in Rome.

3. His statesmanship came to the fore in the **ecumenical scene** when he was appointed Chair of the National Initiative for Evangelism from 1978 until 1983 when it disbanded; it was in this capacity that he was the first Free Church man to address the Council of Bishops in Lambeth. He was Moderator of the Free Church Federal Council in 1986/7, and became Chair of the Churches Together in England Co-ordinating Group for Evangelism. He fronted the ecumenical city-wide missions in York (One Voice) and Plymouth (Making Waves).

4. In **British life** there have been state occasions where he has had a prominent role: in the wedding of the Duke and Duchess of York in Westminster Abbey, at the Service of the Festival of Remembrance in the Royal Albert Hall, leading Bible Studies for Members of Parliament, lunching with the Queen in Buckingham Palace – which incidentally is where he was when his second term as President of the Methodist Conference was announced in the Conference. He addressed a group of High Court judges and barristers, and broadcast regularly on the radio, being known by thousands for his broadcasts of 'Thought for the Day' on Radio Four. (The colleague of one of his sons, having heard him on the

radio that day asked whether his father had a thought every day!). For his services to the country he was awarded the Companion of the British Empire in 1996.

So what were the statesmanlike qualities which ran through these and other facets of Donald's life?

First, there was his strong leadership. It was Donald who transformed a frequently failing football team at Wesley House, Cambridge, into a team which did not lose a match all season. It was his strong leadership which held together as a team the theologically diverse staff of the Home Mission Division for thirteen years. It was his strong leadership which enabled those ecumenical city-wide missions to take place, and it was his strong leadership which was a unifying influence during the turbulent years around his second Presidency. In all the many committees he chaired, he listened attentively to what everyone had to say, succinctly summarised the implications of the different points of view, and usually through his leadership and skill in diplomacy gained some kind of consensus.

Second, he worked strategically. He did nothing without a reason. He joined the Boys' Brigade in Consett in his childhood because it had a football team! He was formative in the lives of many university students through his years as Travelling Secretary for the Inter-Varsity Fellowship. He spent many years training others to be ministers, not as statesman only in this country but in Umuahia in Eastern Nigeria. More recently he was one of the lecturers at the Preachers' Conferences at Cliff College. In these and many other ways he adopted a statesmanlike strategy in order to influence as many as possible.

Thirdly, he was focused. With the heart of an evangelist, his main purpose was to introduce others to Jesus, his Lord and Saviour. This aim lay behind all that he undertook, and nothing gave him greater joy than to see a person develop a living relationship with Jesus.

Fourthly, he was a visionary. Using his penetrating mental skill, while at the Home Mission Division and on its behalf he wrote *"Sharing in God's Mission"*, a theological synthesis of evangelism, social caring and the struggle for justice. More recently he wrote *"Into the 21st Century"*, offering a visionary response to the kind of world we live in and the present state of the Church - a book he had planned to expand.

Fifthly, his statesmanship was shown in his willingness to be vulnerable and to show his deeper feelings. It takes a great man to shed tears as he did when at the World Methodist Council in Singapore in 1991 he expressed penitence for the racist and imperialist attitudes of white, Western people like himself.

Finally, in all areas of his life, he was an encourager. In spite of the many demands on him in the multiplicity of tasks he undertook, he had time for individuals. Perhaps it was because of this that he was so effective as a statesman. As he presided at the British Methodist Conference, as he chaired the World Methodist Council, he could look out on people whom he knew personally, people whom he had encouraged and counselled, some who had stayed within the ranks of Methodism partly because Donald was there. An evangelical statesman who did not flinch from saying what was hard to hear, but who said it with love and compassion; an evangelical statesman who led from the front but gave time to the person struggling at the back; an evangelical statesman whose eyes were fixed on Jesus, the author and perfecter of his faith, for whose honour and glory he devoted his many gifts.

My final sight of Donald was at the Methodist Conference in Scarborough in June 1998. It was the Sunday afternoon and I was about to deliver my Vice-Presidential address. As I glanced around the gallery, I spotted Donald, leaning forwards, beaming at me encouragingly: (for he had encouraged me to stay with it until my turn came). And I could almost hear him say, 'Go for it, Margaret!'.

A fine statesman, with the personal touch. Thank God for Donald English.

The Rev. Dr. Joe Hale, General Secretary of the World Methodist Council assesses Donald English as he knew him on the world stage of the Methodist Church.

Donald English, the World Leader

Like everyone else attending the 13th World Methodist Conference in Dublin in 1976, I was profoundly challenged by Donald English who had been asked to give the Bible Studies. He was still relatively unknown, yet he captivated his audience straightaway. Few speakers can do that, but Donald English did. He was throughout his distinguished career not just a brilliant preacher, but an evangelist who understood and was able to communicate that which lies at the heart of the Christian Gospel in a way which was always clear and convincing.

In his very first study he spoke about engaging people in a world of chaos and darkness with "Christian answers to questions which are being raised". He directly challenged some of the fashionable ways in vogue at the time.

He said, "It seems incredible to me that Christians should talk about wanting to make people more human but not wanting to make them Christian." He went on, "As a Christian I do not understand how full humanity can be reached except in Christ, and it amazes me that so many of our people would rather spend day after day simply doing good to others and not explain that this is all in the service of Jesus Christ. I find that incomprehensible; for if there is to be a removal of chaos and darkness it must surely come through Him who is the Way, the Truth and the Light. To talk about a creator God is not to remove the need for evangelism, it is precisely to underline it".

Dr. English was opening doors to new winds that would blow through the Church. What would crystalize in his heart and mind, he later advocated effectively throughout the world. He became convinced that one urgent need in the Church was an understanding of "Christian Apologetics". In the late 1980s, the World Methodist Council's Evangelism leaders took up this concern which Donald had so forcefully introduced at the World Methodist Conference in Dublin years earlier. Some 200 leaders met at the sites of the "Seven Councils of the Early Church" with the theme - "Apologetics and Evangelism in the Early Church and today."

Lectures were organised at the different places where the apostolic mission in the Mediterranean had begun. Donald had helped to prepare this programme and gave one of the lectures. The final lecture was given at the place where the first Council of Nicea met in 325 AD. From this occasion came "a Call to the Church" partly prepared by Donald, and sent out to Methodist Christians in 93 countries to bear witness to the revelation of God in Christ as declared in the Nicene creed, grounded in Scripture and prayer.

1. to identify intellectual obstacles and objections people have to the Christian faith, seek to understand them and to answer them humbly and modestly at the level at which they are offered

2. under the Lordship of Christ to follow His own example of loving God and serving others as is now possible in the power of the Holy Spirit, released by Jesus' death and resurrection.

This statement characterized Donald English's concern for Christian Apologetics in the clear call from 1 Peter 3.15 - "Always be prepared to make a defence to anyone who calls you to account for the hope that is in you".

One of Donald's powerful lectures during that conference was near to Mar's Hill in Athens where Paul once preached. His presentation encapsulated the great contribution he was then making to the Methodist Church in Britain. We felt that you were beginning to regain momentum and to discover new confidence and hope. In retrospect his words reflected the enormous contribution he was making to world Methodism. For over 22 years he had been closely involved in world evangelism and the leadership of the World Methodist Council.

In Athens he said, "Apologetics concerns saying what we mean in contexts where people are inclined not to believe what we mean, and saying it in a way that they believe it! The task of apologetics in the face of unbelief is to make the Christian gospel clear in a way that defends it against unbelief and presents it in as convincing a way as possible."

In the same address he gave a lively exposition of Acts 17 and explained what was happening between Paul and the Athenians - "Apologetics is beginning where people are with their own perceptions and seeking as far as possible, to lead them through to where the gospel is". Donald English believed apologetics was far more than pointing to Jesus as the clue to the church. Rather he claimed, "It is to point Jesus as the clue to the whole of life". To address a world that does not believe, we must say, "The centre of the universe is the word of God whom we have seen in the face of Jesus Christ".

But there is something more to be said about Donald English. He was not only a brilliant preacher, teacher and thinker. I saw him practise that which he so effectively advocated as we were together in different places around the world. One of those places was in the town where we live. Some years ago Donald was invited to preach in the Sunday morning service in the church we attend. It is a relatively large church of about 1,200 members. All that I have said and quoted in this brief article was apparent that morning. His manner of addressing this congregation, his compelling and convincing argument for the truth of the Faith, his consideration of the people in the congregation and his evident love for God as he knew and experienced Him in Jesus Christ. It was Donald's first visit to this church and he was preaching in a formal service of worship. At the end of his sermon, in the most natural way possible, he invited those who wished that day to respond to the offer of the gospel, to come forward and kneel at the communion rail for prayer. Many moved from the pews where they were sitting, in response. It was electrifying - a memorable moment of truth for all of us present. His message was brought home through the power of the Spirit, and through the personality of the preacher. He was one of the greatest Christian apologists I have been privileged to know. Many gifted speakers have spoken in our church over the years. They have come and gone, leaving positive memories of great sermons. What is still remembered by many is the Sunday Donald English brought a clear and compelling message, and then - in a natural act that grew out of the message that he had preached - gave people opportunity to respond.

Donald English was an original. He was a peerless preacher and teacher. All that he understood and taught others of the principles of Christian apologetics and work of evangelism he demonstrated in his own life and ministry. May God raise up others who will follow him.

The Rev. Martin Turner until recently Chairman of Headway, and Superintendent minister of the Hemel Hempstead and Berkhamsted Circuit, writes about Donald's relationship with those who attend the Annual Methodist Conference, year after year.

Donald English - Mentor

To go to theological college in the radical mid-seventies was a great shock to me. I had been converted, and then joined the local Methodist church, a loving and caring community where the gospel was preached faithfully week by week. That church and circuit was my total experience of Methodism, and I had fondly and naively assumed that Methodism in general would be my local Methodist situation writ large. I was wrong!

In theological college just a handful of students shared my evangelical convictions, and I felt lost and threatened. How thankful I was therefore when I first heard Don English preach, and how thankful when he sought me out to ask how I was faring and to offer me words of advice and encouragement. Thus began a very precious relationship which lasted throughout Don's life, one in which his counsel was a firm compass point from which I could fix the direction for my own journey. Let me try to highlight the key ways in which Don shaped my vision.

He helped me to live on a broad map.

In the sixties and seventies too many conservative evangelical ministers tended to put all their effort into building up their local churches, content to leave the Connexion to get on with whatever it wanted to. Don's decision to found "Conservative Evangelicals in Methodism" was a crucial one, for this group aimed to hold Methodists within the denomination, and to work within the structures to present a Biblical witness and to win influence for that viewpoint. In college Don shared this vision with us, and it was a vision which thrilled us and ensured that we would see our role as one to be played not just in the local church but, as far as we were able, also at District and Connexional level. For me personally this meant that when I was asked to get involved in the sometimes tedious detail of District and then Connexional Committees, I said "yes," and worked hard both to get to know others from different theological backgrounds and to argue carefully my own case and position.

He showed me second best was not good enough.

Whether we were focusing on something personal, academic or spiritual, Don's concern was always that those he saw as possible future leaders within

Methodism should be the very best they could be. This conviction sometimes led to uncomfortable interviews, and I did not always agree with Don in certain areas, but he had the integrity and concern to challenge me and others face to face, and we always respected that. He helped teach me how to be an effective operator within Methodism.

I hope that no one will think it an insult to Don if I say that he was a very tough and wily church politician! Always so gracious and positive, he nevertheless knew exactly what he was about and exactly where he wanted to go. I remember making my first speech at the Methodist Conference and as soon as the session ended Don sought me out to encourage me to speak again, telling me of both the strengths and weaknesses of what I had said and how I had said it. From that occasion right through to Scarborough in 1998 Don always had helpful suggestions about angles to take and points to be picked up; this wisdom was greatly appreciated.

He helped me have a wider vision for Methodism.
Don English took a great deal of criticism over the years. Almost all of it was unfair. Yes, he could be tough and he held what some regarded as far too big an influence, but Don was a humble man at heart and his concern was for the good of the wider Church. I think it fair to say that through his work, and especially through his travels, Don's vision for the Church grew wider over the years. Some evangelicals felt betrayed by this, and the criticism that he had lost his evangelical cutting edge hurt him more than any other.

Others, however, myself included, were greatly influenced by this wider vision. His insight into issues such as poverty and racism both challenged and thrilled us and helped us to live out the faith on a wider map. Also Don would not waste time in sterile theological trench digging. Rather he encouraged us to reach out hands to those who might not agree with every dot and comma of our evangelical theology, but who nevertheless loved Jesus and were working for the coming of the Kingdom.

He showed me how important individuals are.
It was remarkable to be at Don's thanksgiving service and to see the huge range of people there, and on talking to them discover that an almost universal experience was the feeling that Don knew you and valued you as being very special - it was a great gift. One personal example of this was being at the Keswick Convention where Don was the main speaker. I was newly married and Biddy and I were camping in the area and decided to go along. Don saw us at the back of the tent and, although besieged by folk wanting to speak to him when he had finished, sent a message and then took to tea, two young and scruffy campers who felt immensely valued by his care.

In Conclusion

I must say that in Donald English's death I and many others feel we have lost our key mentor, our spiritual father in Christ. For twenty-five years of my ministry Don has always been there; for me such a wonderful source of advice and counsel. The measure of his influence, and the quality of his mentoring, is shown in the fact that evangelicals are no longer on the margins of Methodism. Rather we are gaining our rightful place within the centre. Increasingly our contribution is valued and listened to. Don was used by God to be one of the key people in bringing that about. Our best tribute to him is to keep pressing to bring the Biblical heritage of evangelical Methodism back into the heart of the Church. This is the place where Don put it. This is the place where it belongs.

The Rev.Richard M. Andrew - minister in the Eccleshall Circuit, Sheffield reflects on some of Donald English's books, and his role as a writer.

Donald English - Writer

In a beautifully observed obituary published in The Guardian after Donald's death, Leslie Griffiths suggested that 'Writing wasn't his strong point'. Even the warmest of Donald's champions would not place him amongst the greatest of creative theologians. Yet to leave the matter there would be to do him a great disservice. True, his writing comes to us largely in the form of pamphlets and small books. Nevertheless, the perceptiveness of his analysis and his capacity to make profound truths accessible to ordinary people frequently made his writing a joyful complement to his preaching.

I first read a book by Donald English in 1991 . He had just spoken at a District Rally at the Dolphin Centre in Darlington during his second term as President of the Conference. He was in fine form reeling off a series of Geordie jokes, comfortable in a region which had done so much to fashion his spirituality and sense of vocation. The accompanying roadshow was dominated by a selection of books and pamphlets written by Donald. I bought a book entitled **"Why Believe In Jesus?"**, (Epworth Press, 1986), a series of reflections which began life as evangelistic addresses.

It has all the hallmarks of Donald the writer. It is at once passionate and committed, yet at the same time tempered by wisdom and mature reflection. It is rooted in everyday concerns yet never loses sight of the wealth of the Scriptures and the Christian tradition. It is writing aimed at transformation and conversion yet never seeks to co-erce or manipulate. It is the work of a writing pastor. Donald's talent as a writer mirrored his gifts as a preacher. His writing is perceptive and observant. In turn, these qualities are combined with personal integrity and vulnerable dependence on God. It was these qualities I think that gave him a unique clarity of vision. Yet these talents were exploited in a particular fashion. On the whole Donald's writings were aimed at popular consumption. This is not to denigrate his achievement. Rather the lack of breadth and depth that usually accompanies popular Christian paperbacks gives us an indication of the value of his gifts. Sadly, in recent years, there have been precious few popular mediators of the tradition of the quality of Donald English.

His writings aim at lucidity and comprehension yet never avoid complex theological problems. He was a writer with an enormous respect for learning. He was also a writer with evangelical passion. Yet he never sought to be an evangelical in isolation from the broad streams of Christian faith nor of the contemporary world. Behind each sentence lies a profound grasp of the mystery and of the presence of God in all things. There is much to admire throughout Donald's writings. If pressed, however, I would recommend three books in particular.

The first is **"Sharing in God's Mission"**, (Home Mission Division, 1985). This booklet, which he masterminded, began life as a response to a direction from the Middlesbrough Conference in 1983. It is a beautifully balanced report that bears much study. It provides suitable material for house groups and for wider consultations. Its value lies in the breadth of its sympathies.

Passion for evangelism and concern for justice in God's world are held together in a creative piece of theological synthesis. The first part looks at our understanding of God, the world and the Church. The second section looks at how this theological foundation can be built upon before the final section deals with practical issues about how the Church can adapt its life for mission. It remains an invaluable resource for any church which is seeking to reflect upon its mission and ministry in the world.

A second book I would recommend is Donald's commentary, **"The Message of Mark,"** (IVP, 1992). The Gospel of Mark held a special place in Donald's affections. He describes this commentary, which came after many years of detailed reflection upon the Gospel; as '...the next step in a journey of exploration, a journey which never fails to reveal more than I had discovered before, and to promise even more if I am willing to look beyond what is obvious and to allow it to speak to my own life and setting' (p.10). Reading the commentary reminds us of the keenness of Donald's insight but perhaps more importantly it points us to a writer who retains his sense of wonder and awe before the text and who wishes to move the reader beyond the pages of the commentary to the subject of which they speak. Here is a writer at the height of his powers seeking to bridge the gap between the scholarly commentary and the ordinary reader without losing sight of the importance of simple devotion. It is full of distilled wisdom and practical insights and bears reading in full or in its several sections.

The final book I would recommend is **"An Evangelical Theology of Preaching"** (Abingdon Press, Nashville; 1996). This book represents the pinnacle of Donald's achievements as a writer. Several of the chapters began life as lectures at Asbury Theological Seminary. For the theological beginner it is perhaps the most inaccessible of his writings. Yet it is a book worth persisting with for it brings together the fruit of a lifetime's reflection upon the nature and context of preaching by one who spoke with a rare authority upon these matters.

How then should we assess his achievement as a writer?

Donald's distinctive contribution as a writer lay in his ability to read the intellectual and spiritual currents of the age through an evangelical lens and to translate its implications into a form that could be widely understood. More profoundly he was a writer of vulnerable dependence upon God, who pointed others to Christ, the One in whom Donald had discovered so much.

The Rev. Brian Hoare was part of the team at the Home Mission Division who worked with Donald before he retired. A former President of Conference and tutor at Cliff College, he preached the sermon at the Thanksgiving Service on Friday 2nd October at Westminster Central Hall.

Donald English - Himself

There can be few for whom the name Donald English conjures up no picture at all. Quite apart from his exceedingly wide circle of personal friends and acquaintances, there must be many thousands more who either saw him in person or are familiar with his appearance through photographs or television. A tall, slim, pleasant featured man with upright bearing and athletic figure, neatly and soberly dressed, his once sandy-red hair was latterly thinning and grey giving him a distinguished look. People were immediately put at ease by his open and friendly face, smiling eyes and the welcoming grip of a large freckled hand outstretched in greeting. He was well spoken with a softly lilting voice that gave just a hint of his roots in the north-east of England and was instantly recognisable to thousands who never met him in person but listened avidly to his regular radio broadcasts.

Born in Consett, County Durham in 1930, Donald was the only son of a colliery electrician and his wife, both members of the local Methodist church. He was brought up in that close-knit mining community and was greatly influenced not only by his parents but also by his Junior School teacher, Jack Gair. During his school days Donald developed a great love for football and became (and always remained) an ardent supporter of Newcastle United. As the local Boys Brigade ran a football team, he joined the 2nd Consett Company and it was through the Bible Class under the leadership of the Captain, Matt Atkinson, and the Lieutenant, Bob Dodd, that he came to faith. His minister at that time was the Rev. Benjamin Drewery (whose son, also Benjamin, followed his father into the ministry), and it was he who first took Donald out to help with services around the circuit and encouraged him to become a Local Preacher. Thus in his early years the foundations of his life and ministry were laid.

Donald English's career and achievements are documented in other chapters of this book. But what kind of man was he? What sort of personality lay behind all that he accomplished? Graphologists would have had a field day reading Donald's character from his handwriting! It always had a flow to it; one word often joined to another by a sweeping stroke of the pen. Over the years it seemed to gather a growing urgency and become increasingly illegible, as if he was a man in a hurry whose pen could not keep up with his fertile mind. This was partly due to the mounting pressure of responsibility he shouldered, but was also indicative of the vision which drove him onwards. He was a man of firm evangelical conviction, a sharp and incisive thinker, and a strong personality who knew what he was aiming for and would leave no stone unturned to achieve it. Some indeed misinterpreted his determination as personal ambition. Whilst 'ambitious' is certainly a word which could be justly applied to him and he did seek and grasp opportunities to influence (even to steer) people and events, his ambition was always ultimately for the good of the Church and the furtherance of the gospel rather than for any sort of personal aggrandisement. He was a man of deep Christian commitment, great personal devotion and genuine humility, and the whole dynamic 'flow' of his life was for the greater glory of God.

To get to know Donald English was to discover someone who was genuinely 'a friend to all and the enemy of none' as Wesley put it. He had that happy knack of making you feel you mattered, and in conversation would give you his undivided attention. This even extended to those with whom he profoundly disagreed, for he was always gracious and irenical in spirit. He was a great encourager, and made people believe in themselves – perhaps reflecting what his own schoolteacher had done for him all those years before. Although open to new ideas and second to none in his insistence that we are called 'to serve the present age' and to incarnate the gospel in our own time and culture, he was nevertheless a traditionalist at heart. He enjoyed singing contemporary worship songs, but would more naturally choose the tried and tested hymns of the faith when leading worship himself. He liked things done properly, and enjoyed the pomp and ceremony of events like the opening of the Methodist Conference.

It is interesting to note that until his designation as President in 1978 he had always been known as 'Don', but from then on his signature became 'Donald'. Perhaps he deemed that to be more 'proper'! Those who knew him in his earlier 'Don' days remember him as a fun loving outgoing person with a great sense of humour and a fund of stories for every occasion. His Geordie upbringing had somehow given him a belief in the importance of the ordinary, and he revelled in being with ordinary people, doing ordinary things and enjoying ordinary pleasures. His love of football developed into considerable skill on the field, and he played for the English Universities and for Leicester City. He enjoyed good food, though had fairly traditional tastes, and he and Bertha loved entertaining others in their home. He would relax by listening to music, especially his beloved Mozart (of whose works he had a considerable collection), and loved wandering round art galleries and museums. He read immensely widely in all sorts of fields besides theology, and particularly enjoyed biographies of which he had an impressive number in his library.

It was his family, however, which brought Donald the greatest pleasure of all. He was immensely proud of his two sons, Richard and Paul, and their wives Maxine and Carol, and took great delight in his three grandchildren. He was devoted to Bertha, his Northern Irish wife whom he had married in July 1962. She was a gifted teacher whom he met when she was teaching R.E. in Leicestershire. She later joined the staff at the Methodist College, Belfast. They were demonstrably affectionate when together, and when Donald was away on his travels Bertha's photograph always stood on his bedside table and he would ring her every night to share the day's news. Her death from cancer in 1997 left him devastated, and although his faith remained firm he found the adjustment to life without her almost too difficult to bear. From that perspective it was a blessing that they were so soon reunited in heaven.

On Friday 2 October 1998 over a thousand people gathered in Westminster Central Hall for a Service of Thanksgiving for the life of Donald English. It was a stirring occasion with glorious music and spoken tributes from a galaxy of church leaders. Yet for those who gathered there, and for the many others who were touched by his life, it is not so much his achievements and honours which they remember, impressive though they were. It is rather the person he was: Donald the man, whose life illustrated so well the faith he lived and preached, and who somehow made it so much easier for the rest of us to believe in Jesus.

The Rev. Dr. Billy Graham sent the following personal tribute, which was read out at the Thanksgiving Service held at Westminster Central Hall, London on Friday 2nd March.

"There are so many things that have already been said about Donald English - and there are so many things that I would like to say out of my years of friendship with him - that space does not permit.

Don was one of the greatest men of God I have ever known. His arms were wide open to the fellowship of all believers whatever their denominational background. From my earliest evangelistic crusades in England, he was one of our great outspoken supporters.

He supported us at times when it was not the popular thing to do. He encouraged me so many times by a note, a telephone call, or a word as we would be brought together in some conference. There are very few men in the ministry of any denomination that I looked up to and wanted to emulate like Don English.

He was an evangelist at heart as well as a great teacher and pastor. Like Barnabas, he was an encourager to younger clergy. It is my prayer that God will raise up other men like Don English not only to lead and influence world Methodists, but the entire world Church.

Billy Graham."

SOME IMPORTANT DATES
IN THE LIFE OF DONALD ENGLISH

20 July 1930	Born
1948 - 1953	Student University College, Leicester
1953 - 1955	R.A.F.
1955 - 1958	I.V.F. Travelling Secretary
1958 - 1960	Student, Wesley House, Cambridge
1960 - 1962	Assistant Tutor, Wesley College, Headingley, Leeds
1962	Married Bertha Forster Ludlow
1962 - 1965	New Testament Tutor, Union Theological College Umuahia, Eastern Nigeria
1966 - 1972	Minister, Cullercoats Methodist Church
1972 - 1973	Tutor in Historical Theology, Hartley Victoria College, Manchester
1973 - 1982	Tutor in Practical Theology and Methodism, Wesley College, Bristol
1978 - 1979	President of the Methodist Conference
1982 - 1995	General Secretary, Home Mission Division of the Methodist Church
1986 - 1987	Moderator of the Free Church Federal Council
1990 - 1991	President of the Methodist Conference
1991 - 1996	Chairman of the World Methodist Council
1996	Awarded C.B.E.
28 August 1998	Died

A Letter from the Chairman of Headway, the Rev. Paul Smith, (Superintendent Minister, Altrincham Circuit.)

Dear Friends,

Donald English was one of the founding fathers of Conservative Evangelicals in Methodism. That organisation joined with The Methodist Revival Fellowship some years ago to form Headway. More recently we have welcomed into our membership those who formerly belonged to the Dunamis Renewal Fellowship.

Whilst Headway does not claim to speak for every evangelical Methodist it does represent the distinctive evangelical contribution in the Methodist Church at every level of our Church's life; nationally, at the Conference, in the Districts, with regional and district meetings, and more locally, providing fellowship for evangelical Methodists in both Circuits and local churches.

Donald was the epitome of an evangelical Methodist and demonstrated, by his life and witness, the difference which evangelical Methodists can make to their denomination. He rejoiced at the growth in Headway's membership in recent years and we owe much to the visionary leadership which he provided. The increasing influence of evangelical Methodists within our Church warmed his heart.

We thank God for Donald's life and every memory which we have of him; but he would be the first to remind us that the work must go on. Headway, through its membership and officers, is constantly demonstrating that together we can make a difference. You could be part of that. If the truths for which Headway stands are dear to your heart, if you long for revival in our land and renewal in the Church, if you are grateful for the past but would like to mould the future of our denomination we would like to welcome you into Headway's membership. Membership forms can be obtained from the Headway stand at major Methodist events, or why not write, phone or e-mail the membership secretary-

> Neil Baldock,
> 43, Bath Road,
> Wootton Bassett,
> Swindon, Wilts SN4 7DE.
> tel: 01793 853197   e-mail nrbaldock@aol.com

Welcome!

> Every blessing,
> Paul Smith.